HEY GOD, CAN YOU STOP THE RAIN SO I CAN GET OFF NOAH'S STINKY, SMELLY ARK?

THE RAVEN TELLS HIS SIDE OF THE STORY

D1275709

TROY SCHMIDT
ILLUSTRATED BY CORY JONES

HEY, REMEMBER THAT STORY ABOUT THE SHIP THAT FLOATED AROUND WITH ALL THOSE ANIMALS ON BOARD DURING THAT FLOOD? GUESS WHAT, I WAS A PASSENGER ON THAT CRUISE. AND I KNOW EVERYONE LOVES TO TALK ABOUT THAT STORY LIKE IT WAS SOME COOL FLOATING PETTING ZOO, BUT IT WASN'T.

MY WIFE RITA WON US THIS CRUISE THAT STARTED IN THE BACKYARD OF SOME
GUY NAMED NOAH. NONE OF US KNEW ANYTHING ABOUT HIM, OR WHETHER
HE EVEN HAD HIS CAPTAIN'S LICENSE, BUT HEY, THE TRIP WAS FREE.
AND BIRDS LIKE A GOOD DEAL. THAT'S WHY WE SAY, "CHEAP, CHEAP!"
WE SAW EVERYONE WE KNEW ONBOARD. RALPH AND RACHEL RHINO.
PETE AND PAT PARROT. GENE AND GRETA GAZELLE. BURT AND BONNIE BISON.
AND OF COURSE, DARRYL AND DIANA DOVE. RITA SAYS I'M JEALOUS OF THEM.
HA! IT'S JUST THAT THEY'RE SO HAPPY AND LOVE-Y DOVE-Y ALL THE TIME.
MAKES YOU WANT TO COUGH UP A WORM. BLLEEEHHHHH!

I PRAYED, "HEY, GOD, CAN YOU STOP THE RAIN SO
I CAN GET OFF NOAH'S STINKY, SMELLY ARK?"

GOD ANSWERED, "YOU'RE BETTER OFF IN THE ARK, RAVEN."

"BETTER OFF? AT LEAST AT HOME, I DIDN'T HAVE TO WATCH
FOR YOU-KNOW-WHAT EVERY TIME I TOOK A STEP!"

BUT GOD DIDN'T SEEM TO SMELL WHAT I WAS SMELLING.

"I'M MISERABLE! WHY IS IT RAINING SO MUCH?"

"THE PEOPLE WERE BEING MEAN TO ONE ANOTHER,
SO I WANTED TO START THE WORLD OVER. I DON'T LIKE IT
WHEN PEOPLE ARE MEAN TO ONE ANOTHER."

THEN, AFTER FORTY LONG DAYS, IT STOPPED RAINING. FINALLY! BUT JUST WHEN I THOUGHT IT WAS OVER, WE HAD TO WAIT EVEN LONGER. IT WAS OVER A HUNDRED MORE STINKY AND SMELLY DAYS UNTIL WE STRUCK LAND. HOWEVER, IT WAS JUST A LITTLE, ITTY, BITTY MOUNTAIN TOP. NOT EVEN ENOUGH ROOM FOR A DUCK TO STAND ON. EVERYONE WAS SAD—BUT THOSE DOVES KEPT SINGING.

AFTER A FEW MORE MONTHS, I WAS GOING CUCKOO.
I HAD TO GET OFF THIS SHIP!
SO I FLEW INTO NOAH'S CABIN TO TELL HIM HOW I FELT.

"I HAVE AN IDEA, RAVEN," NOAH SAID, STROKING THAT BEARD.
"I'M GOING TO SEND YOU OUT ON A SPECIAL MISSION
TO SEE IF THERE'S ANY LAND. CAN YOU DO IT?"

FINALLY, SOMETHING TO DO! I'M OUTTA HERE!

SO I SPREAD MY WINGS, AND AWAY I FLEW, FREE FROM THE ARK AND INTO SOME FRESH AIR. I FLAPPED AND FLAPPED AND FLAPPED, RISING HIGHER AND HIGHER INTO THE SKY. IT FELT GREAT . . . FOR ABOUT FIFTEEN MINUTES.

SUDDENLY I REALIZED I WAS GETTING TIRED. AFTER MONTHS OF MOPING AROUND, I WAS OUT OF SHAPE! I FELL FROM THE SKY AND CRASHED ON THE DECK OF NOAH'S SHIP. EVERY FEATHER ACHED ON MY BODY. AND THEN I PASSED OUT.

IT TOOK A DAY TO RECOVER, BUT I WAS READY FOR ANOTHER TRIP. I'D DO ANYTHING TO GET OFF THIS ARK AGAIN!

BUT NOAH THOUGHT I WAS STILL HURTING FROM YESTERDAY'S CRASH LANDING AND ASKED DARRYL AND DIANA DOVE TO BE THE OFFICIAL LAND SPOTTERS FOR THE ARK.

THOSE HAPPY, CHIRPING, PERFECT BIRDS TOOK MY JOB AWAY FROM ME! EVERYONE WAS EXCITED . . . BUT I WAS SHOCKED!

HOURS LATER, DARRYL AND DIANA LANDED ON THE DECK, LOOKING FIT, HAPPY, AND NOT A BIT TIRED.

"WE DIDN'T SEE ANY LAND. BUT THE WATER IS SLOWLY GOING AWAY. WE SHOULD BE ABLE TO LEAVE ANY DAY NOW!" THEY SAID.

EVERYONE CHEERED . . . BUT I WAS SAD. I WAS OUT OF A JOB AND STUCK ON THIS STINKY SHIP FOR WHO KNOWS HOW LONG!

SEVEN DAYS LATER NOAH SENT DARRYL AND DIANA ON
ANOTHER TRIP. LATER THAT NIGHT, THEY RETURNED.
DARRYL WAS CARRYING AN OLIVE LEAF.

"LAND! THERE'S LAND!" DIANA CRIED.

EVERYONE CHEERED . . . BUT I WAS MAD. I WANTED TO
BE THE ONE THAT FOUND THE LAND! THOSE PERFECT
DOVES STOLE MY PERFECT JOB!

SO I WORKED OUT, DOING PUSH-UPS AND SIT-UPS, GETTING READY
FOR THE NEXT MISSION. I WANTED THAT JOB BACK!

ONE WEEK LATER, WITH MY BIRD-SIZED BICEPS BULGING, I MARCHED UP
TO NOAH TO GET MY ORDERS. BUT IT WAS TOO LATE. DARRYL AND
DIANA WERE TAKING OFF FOR ANOTHER FLIGHT.

BUT THEY NEVER CAME BACK. MAYBE THEY CRASHED.
MAYBE THEY FELL INTO THE WATER.
NOT ONLY DID I FEEL SAD, BUT I FELT BAD FOR BEING MAD AT THEM.
THEY RISKED THEIR LIVES SO I WOULDN'T CRASH AGAIN.

THEN I REMEMBERED WHAT GOD SAID. HE DESTROYED THE ENTIRE
EARTH BECAUSE PEOPLE WERE BEING MEAN TO EACH OTHER,
AND HERE I WAS WITH A STINKY ATTITUDE TOWARD THE DOVES.
AND NOW, I COULD NEVER SAY I WAS SORRY TO THEM.

ONE MONTH LATER NOAH OPENED UP THE SHIP AND LOWERED THE BRIDGE.

"GO," GOD SAID. "AND HAVE A NICE FAMILY!"

RITA AND I BUILT A NEST IN A TREE BY THE RIVER. THAT'S WHEN I THOUGHT I SAW A BIRD WITH AN OLIVE BRANCH IN HIS MOUTH. COULD IT BE? YES! IT WAS DARRYL! I THREW MY WINGS AROUND HIM AND GAVE HIM A BIG BIRD HUG.

"I'M SORRY I WAS MEAN TO YOU," I TOLD DARRYL AND DIANA.

"WHEN?" DARRYL ASKED. "I DIDN'T EVEN NOTICE!"

"I WAS JEALOUS THAT NOAH CHOSE YOU, BUT I WAS REALLY TOO WEAK TO MAKE THE TRIP. I SHOULD HAVE THANKED YOU FOR RISKING YOUR LIFE TO HELP US FIND LAND."

WE RAVENS AND DOVES BECAME BEST FRIENDS AFTER THAT DAY.

AND WE STAYED FRIENDS THROUGH RAIN OR SHINE.

THE END.